You Are Perfectly Flawed

...and Rarer than any Diamond!

Tiffany L. Gough

ISBN: 978-1-71695-867-0

PublishNation LLC
www.publishnation.net

Praise for *"You Are Perfectly Flawed . . . . and Rarer than any Diamond"*

"You have written a fascinating account of your goal to help people realize that we are all, 'perfectly flawed!'" *Marge, client*

"Reading this book, is like being a miner and finding fantastic nuggets of golden wisdom on every page. I couldn't stop underlining all of her grace giving quotes. These quotes are now etched on my heart to aid in guiding my life's passion. Tiffany offers gifts and much more on each page. Open up this book and be prepared to receive!" *Priscilla A. George, owner of Interior Excellence LLC and FrenchBeeBoutique.com*

"I just finished reading this book. It is an outstanding piece of work that takes you from reading to feeling as though you are speaking with a friend. The work she has you do is just like a friend helping you think and figure out things for yourself. Her book is a must read that makes you want to have a friend like her in your life. I am already planning to make this a gift for many of my friends and family." *Sheri Clifford, Facebook Group friend*

"This is an amazing book that will help you look at life's obstacles as lessons and help you spin them to see a positive outcome in any situation allowing You to embrace your flaws and change your perception of self. I enjoyed the personable stories and thought-provoking activities sprinkled throughout the book that are designed to help you put thoughts into words in order to analyze what you would like to change and set goals for yourself. The theme of your flaws being like flaws on a diamond helped provide a visual picture in order to drive the point home." *Elizabeth Johnson, Former* Colleague

"Tiffany has a powerful way of writing that will spark a light in your heart while reading her book. She fills the pages with insightful and intimate comments and real-life experiences to draw you in; and addresses issues of the spirit and guides the reader to a better understanding of just how our thoughts impact our lives and experiences. Inviting us all to participate in a journey of self-discovery using worksheets that help bring clarity and as well as to begin making changes to create a better future." *Sandra Gilson, Founder, High-Heeled Go-Givers*

"This well written and timely book is all about how you tell your story. We are all perfectly flawed human beings with all the same needs, wants and desires. This book brings this to the forefront where it should remain in the lives of everyone who reads it." *Cynthia Nolan, Travel Advisor, Expedia*

"It resonates of when comfort is being provided by a source of high intelligence. It is a truly honest and eye-opening story of how to change your perceptions in how you live; an awakening to evaluate how you treat yourself and what to accept while moving forward. Anyone who seeks to be inspired and or need a good uplifting boost of energy needs to read this book!" *Michael Patrick Hoyle, Seattle WA*

"If you've ever struggled with self-acceptance you will find Tiffany's work heartfelt, straight forward and profoundly uplifting. She is a rare light and her story is the hard-earned wisdom of experience which she generously shares in her book. It resonates in a way I will be referring back to for some time to come. Given a chance, you will too!" *Wendy Nelson, Sense Enabled*

"If you know her, you know she herself sparkles and carries that everywhere she goes! A quote I keep with me is when she talks about our formation of character forged out of the hardships in life, "You can't see your diamond being shaped...especially when you are in the midst of being cut." She recounts some intense experiences, and I am awed by her trauma and her will to fight. I can truly picture her as the "Fearless Girl" on Wall Street, hand on her hips and chin up and head held proud." *Carla Vincent, Colleague*

"You are Perfectly Flawed by Tiffany Gough is a lovely book about the Author's life and how she has used difficult times in her past to overcome and be the successful, incredible woman she is today. Tiffany Gough is a successful financial planner in a primarily male industry. Like a diamond, which is nothing of beauty until it is cut, Tiffany reminds us that we all are capable, beautiful and resilient. I highly recommend this book if you are looking for a story of uplifting inspiration. Tiffany Gough's book shines through in her love and how she wants to remind us that we all are diamonds: beautiful, tough, resilient and Perfectly Flawed." *Darcie Guyer, Guyer Benefits NW*

"We all can relate to Tiffany's story in some way. With love and vulnerability, she shows you how to also overcome what you are dealing with in life. You too can become a powerful co-creator in your own life. This book is full of wisdom that is easy to grasp and start to apply in your own life." *Janis Bayley, Metamorphosis Coaching LLC*

TABLE OF CONTENTS

ACKNOWLEDGEMENTS

I would like to thank each and every person who has ever supported me throughout my life and my career.

A special thank you to my parents, Brian and Lynn for your love and support every second of my life! For teaching me and supporting me through all of my challenges. "I'm no show pony...I am a Clydesdale!" Thanks for reminding me of that when I need it! Dad, I love my logo monogram that you designed for me! It is truly amazing just like all of your work! Mom, thank you for your gift of attention to every detail. As well as, the faith to know the things that I am able to change and those that I cannot.

To my friends and family, that have left this Earth; I have felt your strength and your heart! My Grandpa Gordie always called me Typhonnie...as I was a force to be reckoned with! Thanks for recognizing my power and strength early on. I no longer whisper "I am the storm"; I shout it!

To my friends and family, who have supported me along the path; I am so grateful that our paths connected and your love!

Thank you to God and the Universe that you blessed me with everything! And the constant push to keep writing. It is when, I said yes to you, that things fell into place and also got more challenging. It was then, I knew that this book was meant to be in the world...not just inside me!

For my bonus sons, Bobby and Daniel, you were the bonus that came when I married your Dad. I am thankful that you are in my life. I want you both to know that you can do anything you want...the Universe will rise to meet your heart's desire!

And for my husband, Fred, who loves me flaws and all. For your support and belief in me, that I can do anything I decide. I look forward to making the rest of our dreams come true together.

INTRODUCTION

Dear Reader,

You have found this book at the perfect time. It is not a mistake. Everything that has happened, happened at the right time and what will happen will happen at the right time. Some things that you have been through have been very difficult and some have been awesome, and you will experience more of both in the future.

This book almost didn't happen. I struggled with the thought, 'Who am I to write this? I don't have all my shit together.' For a little while, I let fear take over. I was concerned I would be judged, mocked, and ridiculed by many. However, and thankfully, my heart and my clients said, "Your story will help many." It already had helped some. To those who wish to judge me, that is your choice. Your choice has nothing to do with me. You have no power over me and what you think is truly nothing more than your perception of me, me as you decide to see me.

Before I get into parts of my story, I want to explain that I have a passion for helping people and a passion for jewelry and gemstones. I will be using a lot of analogies and stories about these passions to visually bring my story to life.

Definition of faceting (from www.thefreedictionary.com)

"A process of cutting regular planes on a stone in a predetermined pattern that is related to the stone's crystalline structure. The first precious stones used for decorating jewelry were not faceted at all, but smoothed and rounded into the cabochon style (a cabochon is a stone with a flat back and a domed face). It was discovered, however, that some stones reflect more light if they are cut into facets, and so the face was cut into regular planes as in the rose cut. The backs of these early stones were still flat but, through experiment lapidaries learned to shape the bottom of a stone into a point (known as a pavilion) that further increased the gem's fire."

In summary, faceting is a grinding and polishing process (commonly called "cutting") that creates a beautifully finished gemstone suitable for jewelry.

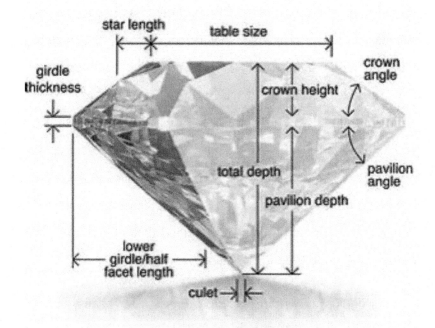

GIA Anatomy of a Diamond (4cs.gia.edu).

Side note - I always wanted to be a Tiffany designer for Tiffany & Company. Well, that did not happen...yet! I would welcome the opportunity should it present itself. Yes, I would love to create a few pieces of jewelry as a side hustle. I will be asking the Universe (God) for that. It is important to know that the Universe will rise to meet your desires.

Now, I want to explain that, while I reference both God and the Universe, this is not a religious book. Here are my thoughts on religion. I like to think of God and the Universe as the great oceans of the world and the rivers are all the different religions/faiths of the world. As you know, the oceans and rivers cover a huge percentage of the Earth and most rivers flow into oceans. So, I really do not care what or who you believe in. How you get to God/the Universe/a Higher Power is your choice...just get there! Hey, even atheists believe that they need to live a good life...regardless of the existence of God. Please be open to the things that you read here and understand that we are all on this Earth at the same time for a reason.

This book was written to help you see your beauty and the rarity that you are. This book exists to help you put your past in the past and to make peace with it while putting the lessons that you experienced to good use.

To make the most of this book, there are activities for you to do scattered throughout. While most of them include places for you to write, I think it is also good for you to have a blank notebook or journal that you can elaborate in. Be open to completing the activities since they serve a purpose. The activities are also highlighted in the Table of Contents in case you need to come back to them later. I will be adding other activities that can be completed to my website in the near future so please be sure to check it out.

Everything in life begins and ends with love. Fight your fight, find your joy, and find your purpose. You are perfectly flawed and rarer than any diamond!

CHAPTER ONE

A Perfectly Flawed Past

All of us have a past. What we choose to relive of our past is our choice. I could write about all the struggles and challenges that I have gone through. However, after much thinking and debating, I decided not to share my whole story in this book. "Why?" you may ask. Because many of the things that I have experienced I have reconciled and forgiven. Giving them new life in my present or future does not make sense. Also, when I have read books about others' stories, whether I mean to or not, I tend to compare their struggles with my past struggles. Their journey is not mine and neither is yours. I once read an article that said that most people grew up in a very dysfunctional family. Many families are filled with various addictions and forms of abuse, some wealthy and some poor. I am not in a place

derstand your life and you are not in a place to understand
ie. Maybe your life wasn't affected by your family, maybe it
as a teacher or a lover that abused you. Sadly, they probably
didn't think anything of it and didn't even know or care that what
they were doing was wrong, leaving you with the outcome of
their few, or many indiscretions and leaving you to reconcile an
unfair accounting of the time.

Regardless of what your story is...please make it a 'was.' I
have shared a few of my stories throughout this book to help
explain this concept. I left out the gross stuff that no one really
wants or needs to read. I think that if you are going through your
own stuff - reading about other people's trauma can bring you
more harm than peace. Sometimes reading about others' trauma
can lead to you experiencing PTSD. But, sometimes it is good to
know that you are not alone in your struggles and your fight.
That is why I am sharing some struggles with you. The last thing
that I want to do is to bring more stress to your life.

I will tell you that I often refer to myself as the lady with nine
lives...much like a cat. In authoring this book, I have counted
that I am on my eighth life. Who knows how much of my eighth
life I have left? Since I am not truly a cat, will I be granted a
ninth life? None of us are granted time without paying for it in

some way. We are not guaranteed the time that we think we should have. Every second is a gift and should be treated as such. Time quickly slips through the hourglass as each grain of sand goes from the top to the bottom. I have an hourglass on my desk at home. Sometimes I need to sit in silence and turn it over. I listen to the sand as it drops grain after grain... being fully present in the moment and alive!

For Your Notes:

4

CHAPTER TWO

Labels as Flaws

Labels are classifying phrases or names, attached to a person or thing, that are often restrictive or inaccurate. There are thousands of labels out there in the world, bracketing countless people and things into limiting ideals. Here's the thing. Labels are just labels, and they don't define you, though they might try.

As long as we have been on Earth, labels have been in existence. They have existed in every society for as long as society has existed. Labels are not designed to be evil; just like stereotypes are born from certain truths. Labels can even be good such as being passionate, caring, or strong. But, over time, labels have become something of a stigma and people get distraught over them. Having said this, it is one's choice whether labels define them. You must choose the positive ones and leave the negative ones as they do not serve a purpose.

Many people are choosing to limit themselves based on their labels. For some reason, society has let labels determine their competence and limit their options. I especially see these traits when parents talk about their kids. "Oh, my son/daughter has ADHD/ADD, he/she can't do this or that." Labels are something that many people quickly, and even proudly, take on, almost as much as I would gladly put on a Chanel suit. These labels give the illusion that there are restrictions in the competence and ability to do certain things, some especially important things. Although people mean well, they quickly put each other in mental cages.

I was diagnosed with audio, visual and kinesthetic dyslexia as a teen. The truth is, once you know what your labels are, you can learn how to work around them and create diverse ways to handle things. What I've seen is that, oftentimes, when people discover that they have a new label they stop and decide that there is something they can't do. A script, based on their label, begins to be internalized and repeated. Thus, self-inflicted limits in everyday life are created...destined to repeat themselves over and over again.

For one minute, think about all the diamonds in the world. Even they have flaws. Some of the flaws can be seen by the naked eye, while others can only be seen under extremely high magnification. These flaws can be a defining factor in how the stones are cut, and, ultimately, what shape they will have. However, if the same flaw, or same label, is continuously cut, rather than the diamond, or you, being shaped, half the size of the stone, and thus half of the value, will be lost.

What are you doing to cut off what society has thought to be "not normal" about you? What are you doing to not be defined by your labels? Remember that you are perfectly flawed. People either tend to spend their whole lives never fully understanding themselves and their labels or get lost and stuck in the ideals of their labels, never truly realizing their full potential. This is exactly what labels do; they deceive you, making you believe that you are capable of much less than you are.

I work in an industry doing something I thought I could never do, something I was told that I could never do. Teachers, listen up, as your words are very impactful, whether positive or negative. I was told all through school that I was stupid, lazy, and would not amount to anything. One teacher was even so low as to tell me, "Don't even think about college, because it will be a waste of money. You probably won't even graduate high school. You're truly only meant to be here to be barefoot and pregnant." Not very encouraging words for an impressionable mind. If only they had known the hours I spent doing my homework, reading and rereading the same pages over and over again trying to understand; the countless hours spent writing papers and figuring out the algebra and all the other math I have never used since.

Labels do have the potential to be good for naming problems so they can be worked on. During my high school entrance exam, the school administration invited my parents in to discuss some of the problems they saw. At that point, I had to take another test. Oh, how I disliked tests. In most cases, I failed. No matter how hard I tried, I tended to fail; I was a failure based on a self-inflicted script gotten from a label. However, this test was an IQ test, based on numbers instead of a pass-fail grade. I was still not happy taking the test, as I was sure that I would not do well, but I had to do what I had to do. From the results of this test, for the first time in my life, something really positive was revealed about me. It was something that I didn't know, something I could never have previously believed because it was something I was never told. I learned that I have a rather high IQ, I just learn very differently than others. What? I was actually smart? You mean to tell me all those teachers were wrong? I was pretty blown away. This was a turning point for me, and I thank my parents. They did not give up on me but pushed and pushed me because they believed in my potential.

Here is where most stop doing whatever it is that is difficult in their lives because it doesn't come easy as they think it should. I heard all the time that because of my dyslexia I couldn't do this and I couldn't do that. I've known people that have dyslexia who live on state aid because they would rather just say that they can't work because of their impairment. Countless people live in a bubble of belief, that because of their label, there is nothing to be done but be a victim.

This doesn't only occur with dyslexia but with other labels as well, labels that society sees as handicaps. Martin Luther King Jr. proved that a black man could make a difference in America; Oprah Winfrey has proven that women, regardless of their hardship, can go as far as they can dream. There are countless examples of disabled athletes who refuse to let their bodies break their spirit but rather persevere and beat the odds regardless of the labels and stigma that has been attached to them.

I graduated in 1987. Thirty years later, the teacher who had taught me coping skills to help overcome some of my difficulties, told me that in all her years of teaching, I was the worst dyslexic case she had ever seen. She was amazed at all my accomplishments. Did I fail along the way? Oh yes, definitely. I had to find new ways to do things and new measures of success. I don't dwell on my dyslexia or all the other issues that I have. I see them as problems to be solved and overcome if I'm going to live a fulfilled life.

I read the best upside down. This is something that I figured out on my own. My mind flips numbers and letters, making it harder for me to read and understand them. One day I tried reading upside down and found out it helps. However, in this day and age, you can't flip a computer upside down! To be in the field that I am, as a financial advisor, I had to pass a very lengthy exam on a computer, which I did.

While I work with numbers all day long, I often think of my dyslexia as a superpower! I see things differently than many other people do. Maybe your flaws, unknown to you, are your superpowers too. You are special and unique in your own way, with your own potential. While you might need to dig a little deeper than others to find your superpower, trust me...the loot is priceless.

CHAPTER THREE

The Diamond Process

How did you learn a diamond was valuable? Some of us were taught this as little kids by our parents because we were shown either our mom's wedding ring or other jewelry with a diamond in it, and we heard all the beautiful stories. "A diamond is forever," is the powerful marketing ad created by De Beers, making diamonds a symbol of love and commitment.

In actuality, the very first wedding ring was just a simple gold band. The golden band has no beginning or end, symbolizing couples' love. Later on, a ruby was added to symbolize the heart's love. Today, the diamond is a symbol used to profess the everlasting nature of one's love to a significant other.

Imagine if you were at a diamond mine or the Crater of Diamonds State Park in Arkansas and you found a large diamond. Would you put it in your sock drawer and forget about it or would you value and treasure it? I hope your answer is to treasure it and, if it is, why do you not do the same with yourself? Too many of us value so many things other than ourselves when we are truly an original work of art.

I believe that, when we are born, we are like that funky, misshaped diamond, uncut and raw. While people like to say that newborn babies are beautiful, in reality, very few babies are incredibly beautiful at birth. I can feel moms getting mad at me right now, but I can't help the truth. Regardless, every baby grows into themselves and becomes cute and, eventually, beautiful. This process is something that cannot happen without time. As we grow, the facets of our lives make us into the shape we are meant to be. This does not mean we will not have flaws. Every one of us will have flaws, just like the most beautiful and valued diamonds. Some of a diamond's flaws can be seen with the naked eye while others cannot, similar to our flaws. Every flaw in a diamond is a part of it and is one of the things that makes it unique. Similarly, our flaws are part of what makes us who we are and should be cherished and respected. Flaws and all, we must love ourselves; just as we expect our spouses, family members, and loved ones to do. Love starts with us.

Ask yourself, if you were a diamond, beautiful and precious, yet full of flaws, would you throw it away or accept it, flaws and all? Your answer to this is especially important. While others may not see your value, that all the flaws you have are just cuts in the grand shape of a beautiful diamond, your true worth, that's okay. Perception is key in life. As long as you see your true worth, that you are the Aladdin to your story, "the diamond in the rough," then what other people choose to see doesn't matter.

What really matters is what you choose to see. The problem that a lot of people have is that they focus on their flaws and refuse to see their true worth. I don't blame anyone who thinks like this, because in times when life cuts us, when we are going through hard times that lead to self-loathing, it is easier to see the flaws and forget the amazing things about ourselves. Our low points in life make it hard for us to appreciate the good in life and, most importantly, the good in ourselves. But, it is empirical that we see our worth and our beauty.

You may not realize this, but every single trial in your life happens for a reason. Every cut in your life has a reason for being there. What is really important to understand is how amazing you are when you're going through them. You know, for years I wondered why I was going through all the things I was going through. I remember not understanding why I was experiencing some really horrible things and trying to figure it out. I have always tried to figure things out.

I have to tell you, in life, and even in my line of work as a financial advisor and wealth manager, I help people through horrible circumstances, some that I've even gone through myself. Who knew at the time when I was going through those things that someday I would be in the capacity that I would use the lessons I learned to help others? I want you to remember this when you are going through your faceting. You can't see the reasons yet. You can't see your diamond being shaped. You can't understand the reasons for everything, especially when you're in the midst of being cut.

You must have faith in the grand scheme of things. You have to know that if you choose to relive the hardships that you have gone through and refuse to move on from them, all you do is continue to cut your diamond in the same place. Here is a visualization for you. Have you ever tried cutting a piece of paper into a shape and to make a straight line you keep cutting more and more paper off until you have to get a new piece of paper or cut a completely different shape? The same thing happens when faceting a diamond...one little mistake and new decisions need to be made on what size and shape can be made without losing too much of the stone.

You must make a conscious effort not to let past hardships define you, not to let your mind be consumed by them. The purpose of hardship is for us to learn from it and, hopefully, help other people get through their own. Some cuts take longer to heal, there is no doubt about that. But, at some point, you have to move past the experience and leave it in your past, then you can later realize the purpose of the cuts as you look back on the story of your life. The beauty that the cuts create makes a diamond worth much more.

You are rarer and worth more than any diamond; there is no person out there just like you, not a soul that could replace you. The key is to embrace this because life is too dark if we don't realize the light within us.

For Your Notes:

CHAPTER FOUR

Find Your Love

The definition of love is an intense feeling of deep affection (www.lexico.com). The Bible talks about the many characteristics of love. It says love is patient, kind, does not envy, and keeps no record of wrong (1 Corinthians 13), just to name a few. It says "faith, hope, and love; and the greatest of these is love" (1 Corinthians 13:13). As you read this, what do you think about when you read the word love? Is it love from your parents or partner? Love from your kids? Well, while all these are important, the love that I'll be discussing is love for yourself! Everything begins and ends in love with loving yourself.

What does love mean to you personally? Stop for a moment and imagine you were alone on this planet. Everything in existence, the water, the food, the land, the Wi-Fi, all of this is at your disposal to do with as you please. Naturally, you are likely to easily gravitate towards the things that you love, especially since there is no one there to judge you or limit you or even make you work for them; maybe you already know what they are. You would have full authority to find happiness in whatever you wanted with no stigma or boundaries of any kind, you would have full creative control of your life. What would you love and be filled with? How would you take advantage of this experience? Write these things down because they are particularly important. Make a list of all the things you've thought of, all the experiences you would love to have if the world was your oyster and you had full creative control.

Activity #1: Things and Experiences I Love

Things you would love to do:

❖

❖

❖

❖

After you write down things you want to do, number them in order of importance or urgency.

What would make you truly happy:

❖

❖

❖

❖

After you write what would make you truly happy, number them in order of importance or urgency.

Now, reality check. You are not alone on this planet, there are people all around you. You have to share Earth with more people than you will ever meet, a society with often insensible rules, norms, and expectations. How do you still find love for yourself? How do you have love overflow from you and into the lives of the people around you?

Instead of loving yourself and finding time to figure out what you truly love, everyone else's needs tend to come first, your partner's, children's, family members', friends' and other members of your local network, and you get whatever time is left. This is not a good idea. Now, don't get me wrong, I'm neither saying nor implying, that you should not love others or show them affection. In fact, as the social creature that you are, it is important that you have healthy relationships with those you deem important, those you love, and any healthy relationship, whatever form it comes in, requires work and dedication. The point I'm trying to get across is that you need to love yourself first and foremost. A popular quote from the Bible says, "Love your neighbor as you love yourself" (Matthew 22:39), but this can't work if you don't love yourself in the first place. You can't expect others to make you happy if you are unable to find happiness for yourself. You must first love yourself, then you will have lots of love for others.

If you had a coffee date with a friend, do you show up bathed, dressed, and excited to see him/her? You would probably want to smell and look nice for the other person and be attentive to the things they have to say. You would compliment them on their looks and make them feel comfortable in your presence.

Do you go on a coffee date with yourself? I'm talking about getting up, getting dressed and taking yourself to a coffee shop or somewhere else fabulous, just to be present and enjoy the moment and your own company. Or do you stay at home in your dirty pajamas, sitting on the couch and scrolling through social media? The problem is that you are not taking time for yourself. If you would show up for your friend looking your best and on your best behavior, freely and excitedly, why would you not show up for yourself with a similar approach and enthusiasm? Why would you not take the time for yourself?

Now, taking time for yourself could mean something different for you. Maybe a coffee date isn't how you would treat yourself. Maybe you would love to go on a road trip or take a cooking class. Maybe you would love to go to a party because you are a dancing machine and love to be the life of the party. It doesn't matter what it is, most things in life are relative, especially seeing that we are all different. The important part is that you treat yourself, that you don't get so caught up in living everybody else's version of you that you forget what you love and what makes you happy. Take a good look at the lists from the previous pages and ask yourself, "Why can I not do or enjoy these things in the world I live in, in my reality?" There is nothing stopping us from getting the best out of the lives we have. I would argue that the only thing stopping us is ourselves.

It is important that you slow down occasionally and take care of yourself. If you forget to love yourself and only focus on the people around you, you are not honoring yourself. Love yourself every day. Love everything about yourself. If you don't, then it is time for some tough changes or your perceptions of yourself will become your reality. Remember, you are in control of making changes that you see fit. You do not need to change for those around you because they want you too!

Experts estimate that the average person has between 60,000 and 80,000 thoughts every single day. Remember that thoughts are powerful; "As a man thinketh in his heart, so is he" (Proverbs 23:7). Thoughts are not empty, they bear fruit. What you think about becomes your reality; what you think about, you become. If you fill your head with thoughts of being unlovable, unworthy, incompetent, or just not good enough, that is exactly what will happen and manifest in your life. Those negative thoughts plague your mind and soon become your reality. At some point, it doesn't matter what the reality of your potential is or how much people see in you, you will be stuck in the cages of your mind, cages built by your own hands. Self-loathing can be extremely dangerous to both our mental and physical health. Would you not rather see how magnificent and brilliant and amazing and rare you truly are? Failure to do so squanders all the goodness the world has to offer.

Sit in front of a mirror and be thankful for all the amazing qualities you have - whether it is your hair, your eyes, your skin, your smile. View and embrace yourself as the Creator would. Doing so becomes an act of communion with Creation and the Universe and what is more beautiful than that?

Write down what you see that you love in the spaces below. Here are some things to get you started. This is not an exhaustive list. Write down, "I love my smile," "I love my laugh," "I love my hair," "I love my voice," "I love myself."

Activity #2: What do I love about ME?

Look at your eyes (they are the window to your soul). What do you love about them?

Look at your lips and mouth. Listen to your voice (they take nourishment, speak volumes, kiss, smile). What do you love about them?

Look at your nose (it smells the rain, the sweet flowers, and so much more). What do you love about your nose?

Look at your skin (it covers and protects you. Do you have freckles or a warm glow?). What do you love about your skin?

Look at your hair or, if you are bald, the lovely shape of your head (your head holds your amazing brain). What do you love about your hair, head?

When you go to bed tonight, think of all the things that you love about yourself as you close your eyes and begin to dream. Remind yourself of all the beautiful things that you wrote about yourself. Remember that not only is your relationship with yourself more important than your relationship with any other person on Earth, but it is the relationship that all other relationships are built upon. How you choose to love yourself sets the tone on how others will love you. If you clearly do not respect, love, and honor yourself others will see that it is okay for them to do the same. What tone are you setting for all of your relationships?

For Your Notes:

28

CHAPTER FIVE

Find Your Fight

I almost titled this book "Find Your Fight," but there were a lot of other things I wanted and needed to share in this book. Although "Find Your Fight" is always a large part of the book the title did not encompass the entire message of this book. So, because the other aspects of this endeavor such as "Find Your Joy" and "Find Your Purpose" are significant parts of my message, "Find Your Fight" is but a small part of a bigger picture, a cut in the grand design of the diamond that I hope this book will be. Finding your fight is a vital part of this book because I find doing so to be powerful, and I hope that the concept of "Find Your Fight" speaks to a lot of people.

Usually, "the fight" is a response to something that's happened to you, something that has made you fight in one way or another. The fight could have revolved around your life or your health, your kids or your family, something that required you to struggle against the tide. You hear stories of people who are put in situations where they have to display their resilience, like a mother lifting a car to save her child, where there is no way she could have done that in any other situation. The explanation for this is a rush of adrenaline, but you can't run on adrenaline all the time. You must choose what battles to fight and which to let go. Only you can decide what is really important to fight for.

In this chapter, I will talk about my sledding accident that almost took my life. In preparation for writing this chapter, I drove to see the fire hydrant that I ran into, the place where my life changed so dramatically; it's only a block away from where my parents still live. I looked at it. I walked up to it and touched it. Yes, it's a regular old fire hydrant. No, it's not alive. But it stands for such a pivotal point in my life. It represents not only the pain that I went through and the scars that it gave me but also the fact that I overcame such a challenging time. That fire hydrant is proof that I have fight in me.

I got back in my car and looked at the massive hill. If you're not from Seattle, you might not know what kind of hill I'm talking about. You know those movies where they show the streets of San Francisco? This is one of those hills. If you take your foot off your car's brake, the speed you would descend at would be high, so you can only imagine what it was like to be on a sled. Now, back to the fire hydrant story.

One very snowy night in Seattle, many years ago, my uncle, cousin and I decided to go sledding on the hill the next street over from our house. Side note – do not sled on city streets! There are way too many obstructions: parked cars, fire hydrants, etc. Please go to a park when the snow hits the city that you live in. My experience with sledding on a city street could have had a very different outcome.

Let me set the scene...

The snowfall in Seattle that year was some of the highest on record...everything was covered in snow...truly everything! At the time, I didn't know how snowfall changes depth perception the way I do now. I just knew there was a lot of snow, a white playground to play in. My uncle, cousin, and I were all excited to go play in the snow! We spent all day into the early evening walking up the massive hill and sledding down it repeatedly. I was getting tired and decided I was going to go down the hill one last time because my short legs were getting very tired. I climbed up the hill and started my descent.

During my descent, I somehow blacked out. My sled got in a rut and I headed into a fire hydrant headfirst. Crash! I was knocked out for a while. When I finally came to, I noticed the beautiful white snow covered in my red blood, blood that was quickly covering more snow by the minute. I was so cold, and I couldn't get warm. People kept coming up to me and the look on their faces said it all. They asked how I was, and I told them I was cold and couldn't warm up. They all started covering me with their coats. However, I was laying on solid ice and no matter how many layers of coats were laid on me I still couldn't get warm.

There was so much snow and ice that the fire department that was only a block away had to drive to the flattest area of the city. Only then could they come up the street to get me. The fire department took over 45 minutes to get to me. By then, I had lost a lot of blood and my body temperature and blood pressure had gone way down. I was deep in hypothermia, my veins had shrunk down/collapsed, my heartbeat was slow, and I was confused and tired. I just wanted to sleep. The paramedics were struggling to get an IV into any vein. They desperately wanted to run warm fluids to help bring my body temperature up and give me much needed blood to replace what I had lost.

The ambulance took me to Seattle Children's Hospital. As they drove, I went in and out of consciousness. I was cold and bleeding everywhere. At one point, I remember being out of my body and looking at myself. It was not a pretty sight to see because there was blood everywhere. I was bleeding from multiple places and the paramedics were trying many different arteries in an attempt to place a needle. They tried my neck, my hands, my feet, and my legs, everywhere.

I had lost a lot of blood and my pretty ash blonde hair was matted with blood. My skin was a bluish color and there was dried blood on my face. The sight and smell were overpowering. I was so cold and the smell of that much blood was more than I could take.

As I write this, almost 40 years later, I am transported back to that time. When I was looking down on my body...I didn't feel the cold, nor could I smell the scent of my blood. It was like I was watching TV and the sound was distorted. However, there were moments where I could clearly hear the sounds as the paramedics and then the doctors at the hospital worked on me...the beeping of alarms and machines, the buzz of the electric shaver as they cut away my beautiful hair...matted with blood and hiding the damage that the fire hydrant had done. My freshly shaved, matted hair now covered the trauma room floor. The extent of my injury was now in plain sight, clearly showing how much care it needed and how much blood needed to be put back into my body. At this point, I realized I was also bleeding from my throat.

My mind started to wander. On one hand, I could stay on Earth with this messed up and broken body and see where I ended up. On the other hand, I had the choice to go into the light. The light that I saw during my out-of-body experience was so beautiful and peaceful. Also, my grandmother had died the year before and I wasn't scared of letting go.

Then I heard..."She's got to want to fight." It was clear at that moment that it was not my time. God was not done with me and fight I did!

Before authoring this book, I had never shared my experience of seeing the light with anyone. At 11 years old, I had never heard of such a thing happening. Everything that was going on was a lot to process. While the trauma of the experience makes it very painful to relive, the light of the story makes the experience beautiful. When my parents asked me why I never told them about seeing the light, I told them that I felt like they had gone through enough and them knowing that would have been too much. I wanted to protect them.

My experience resonates with "Terrible Beauty Had Been Born," a poem by William Butler Yeats. I experienced a terrible trauma that required a lot of recovery, both physical and mental. And yet, during the trauma, I saw the light and chose to fight. My fight was born and I have been fighting ever since. I have always felt that part of that light came back with me when I chose to fight for my messed-up body that day. It is peaceful knowing that something more exists than our physical form. Whatever you believe, whether it is in God, in the Universe, in a Higher Power...just believe. Even though I did not choose to go into the light at that moment...one day I will.

I remember my mom later told me that the doctor told her that I was the number one trauma of the night. He told them to be prepared for the worst, that they would be taking their daughter home one way or the other, but he was not sure which way. I was my parents' only child, their miracle child. They had a tough time having a baby, so I can only imagine what it must've been like for my parents to hear those words. My mother prayed; it was all she could do. I somehow fought; God wasn't done with me. Thankfully, my time and my diamond were not yet finished.

The fire hydrant incident was just one of my nine lives. A lot of us have experiences where we must choose to "Find the Fight." Some experiences where you need to fight are not as obvious; some are not as clear as choosing life or death. There have been many things that I've experienced that were really bad, experiences that taught me to fight. But those experiences did not break me nor define me; they can only have power if I choose to let them. If you keep thinking about past traumas and painful events and reliving them in your thoughts, you are choosing to give them life and, more dangerously, they are taking away from your present life. Don't dwell on them; they are in your past and the only person that can give them life in the present is you. Like most other things in life, they can't hurt you now unless you choose to let them.

I'm going to say something that you'll probably think is nutty. I want you to say, "Thank you," to all the things in your life that you condemn because without them you wouldn't be who you are right now. You might not be the gift to the world that you are today. The pain you experience can be a catalyst in your life;

what you choose to apply it to is completely up to you. Even heroes have things happen to them that seem completely out of their control. What makes them so incredible is not their super strength or their cool gadgets but their resilience in the face of seemingly unbeatable odds. We might not have time machines or superhuman intellect, but we don't need those things to be our own heroes. All we need to do is put up a fight in the face of adversity. We all admire that spirit, that fight in fictional heroes, but we all have that fight in us as well. I am going to tell you once again, you are worth fighting for, so don't stop fighting.

For Your Notes:

CHAPTER SIX

Find Your Hope

When you let memories of past experiences live with you, more room is made for them to repeat themselves in your present life. I've said this before, but I will repeat it again because it is imperative that you understand this: Whatever you focus on will expand and manifest in your life. You may have heard this said in some other way before. No matter how it is worded, the concept still rings true. Dwelling on specific thoughts, whether good or bad, gives them the power to manifest in your life. "As a man thinketh, so is he" (Proverbs 23:7). This is not a lie. If you let things consume your mind, soon enough they will define you, and all you will see when you look in the mirror are scars.

What consumes your mind? Do you think, "I don't want to hurt anymore," "I don't want to trust anymore," "I don't want to feel anymore?" Well, these ideas will keep coming up because you're feeding them, you're helping them grow. This, in turn, stunts your growth. The next time you think about the rough stuff that has happened in your life, focus on the good things that came out of it. Most of us have had bad stuff happen in our lives on a multitude of scales and occasions. You might find yourself feeling overwhelmed by these events or circumstances. If one looks hard enough, there is usually a glimmer of hope that comes out of tough times. It might take some effort to find it, but for most, the glimmer is the lifeline that is needed to stay sane and find joy. The glimmer could even be the difference between life and death. Therefore, we must see the glimmer of hope in every situation and dwell on that instead of the overwhelming darkness. This gives us the strength to fight and allows us the ability to find happiness afterward.

Sometimes the glimmer of hope is not apparent; sometimes it takes years to surface, while other times the glimmer stares you in the face. In either case, we must make a conscious decision to focus on hope. If you persist, with time, you will begin to see the beauty that has unfolded in you. I plead with you to not focus on the darkness but instead focus on the things that bring you happiness and joy.

People wonder what my secret is. Well, this is it. My secret is not having a perfect life or a stress-free environment because, clearly, I do not have either of those. My secret is my outlook, what I choose to dwell on, and what I choose to release and forgive. When I was a little girl, I used to have a button that said: "I believe in God because of rainbows." Do you remember the first time you saw a rainbow or the first time you saw the waves on a beach? Those waves have been going back and forth on the ocean for millennia. The ocean is a significant place for me. Whenever I find myself in a stressful or troubling situation, when everything is seeming to crumble, in those moments of self-doubt and worthlessness, I picture myself on the beach. I think about standing on the beach with the ocean before me and my feet in the sand. I imagine looking down and watching the waves lapping over my feet and hearing the seagulls. For me, it could even be raining and I would still have a wonderful time at the beach. Whether it's wet, hot, or noisy, I find peace and hope in the experience.

I want you to think about your 'ocean.' Think about a memory from your past or a place that takes you away from your troubles, a place where you can just enjoy the moment and feel peace. If you don't have a place or a memory like this, I implore you to go out and find it because it helps.

It's really important that, as much as you can, you write down the details of memories that fill you with hope. Capture a couple memories on the following pages. Jot down the details of your experiences: the smells, the sounds, the sights, the feel, the calmness, the peacefulness, or even the adrenaline rush, of it. Write down what you were wearing, who you were with, or even include a picture of the event if you have one. It's your job to write down as many memories as you can because it's going to be important for the next part of the activity.

Activity #3: Memories that Bring Peace and Hope

Memory #1

How old were you?

What were you wearing?

Where were you?

Was anyone with you?

What did it smell like?

Were you warm or cold?

Were you wet or dry?

Was the place quiet or loud?

What or who brought you peace?

Do you have a picture or a memento?

What else can help you return to that moment of hope when you need to?

Memory #2

How old were you?

What were you wearing?

Where were you?

Was anyone with you?

What did it smell like?

Were you warm or cold?

Were you wet or dry?

Was the place quiet or loud?

What or who brought you peace?

Do you have a picture or a memento?

What else can help you return to that moment of hope when you need to?

Any other memories? Right them down in your journal.

The truth is life is full of challenges. The pain and discomfort that you have had in the past will come up again, possibly in a different form, a different context or, maybe, you keep reliving past moments.

You might find yourself in uncharted territory that leaves you feeling hopeless or helpless. In those times, joyful and happy memories will make a difference. You know those negative thoughts that keep creeping into your mind? Maybe it's the times you convince yourself of your incompetence. Maybe it's the hurtful things that have been said to you. Maybe you are depressed and you think you can't get through it. Maybe you're dealing with an illness that is consuming your every waking moment, consuming your reality, it's all you can think about. It is in these moments that the happy and joyful memories you jotted down are important. If you can switch gears and think of the love, joy, and happiness that you have experienced and that exists in your life, it sets you down a different path, one toward healing and hope.

In all honesty, I just want to reach out to everyone, give them a big hug. That is what I hope this book is to you, a big hug filled with encouragement and love. I know that there is so much bad in this world: horrible things and circumstances, horrible feelings and illnesses, and even horrible people. All this bad can be overwhelming and can dampen your will to push on, however I want you to remember that your life is worth fighting for and there is always hope.

Remember, when I talked about the diamond story earlier? I've used that story with friends, family, and even clients. A lot of people have thought I was a little crazy when I told them they are rarer than any diamond in the world, that there is not another one of them in the present, past, or future.

One time I told someone my diamond story and I gave them a little acrylic diamond to keep. He clearly thought I was crazy but took the little acrylic diamond that I gave him and put it in his pocket to take home. I could tell that he thought I was a little out there, but that's okay because this is me. This is who I am, and I'm not backing down on who I am. So, time passes and I get a phone call from him. He asked if I had some time to talk, to which I replied: "Of course." He started by telling me about the things in his life that weren't good. He told me that one night, when he was feeling devastated and unloved due to things going on in his life, he was sitting on the floor with a gun in his hand. He then went on to say, "Remember when you told me I was rarer than any diamond? Well, I looked up and saw that little diamond sitting on the counter. I kept it," he said. "I thought it was a little weird, but I kept it." At that moment, he said he put the gun away because he realized that what he was going through was not worth his life, it was just another painful cut in his diamond.

This is true for all of us when we feel like our problems are bigger than we can bear. In our lowest moments, it's hard for us to remember that our lives are bigger than our problems, it's hard to find hope. It's in these moments that we need hope the most. I feel like if I can help anyone, in any way, through these words, then it would be a disservice not to use them.

Words are powerful and your thoughts even more so. What I ask of you is, if you thought of a special "peace and hope" moment, that you bring it to mind when you find yourself in the darkness. Bring to mind hope in the moments when it is not easy to see that you are fighting for life or death, in those moments of struggle — bring to mind something that reminds you that it is worth it to keep fighting. Part of the fight is to keep out the negative thoughts because those are more dangerous to you than you think. I want you to choose hope over fear and every other negative thing handed to you in life.

For Your Notes:

CHAPTER SEVEN

Find Your Joy

I know it seems weird to talk about joy after what I just narrated, but as I said before, these chapters in our lives do not and should not define us. These chapters only hold the power and significance that we allow them to have. What we take from them is our choice. Life is mostly about choices. It's easy to look upon these memories and see nothing but darkness and pain, but if you choose to think about traumas and be grateful that you have made it through them; if you look upon your scars and find peace, see that you have the fight to withstand any and all other things that could come your way, there you will find joy.

Imagine if you woke up every morning filled with joy, the kind of joy that you had as a child. Remember when you were younger, and you knew you could do anything?!? You were afraid of nothing. When did you lose that? Whenever it happened, I want you to forgive whoever or whatever stole your JOY! You have harbored resentment inside you for too long.

When you harbor an enemy in your heart, the hate or anger you have towards them damages you more than you know. The negative feelings also block you from what you are meant to achieve in your life. You have a mission that only you can do. If you die before you do it...it dies with you. Think about that for a moment. Really let that sink in.

People always want to know why I'm so full of joy; they think my life is and has been free from problems and traumas. The thing is, I choose joy because life is way too short. I've experienced eight of my nine lives. I joke, but seriously, I shouldn't even be in this world anymore. For me, joy is not just a state of mind, it's also a brand. I look at JOY as Jesus first, Others second and myself (Yourself) last. This keeps integrity in my heart, and there is never a question of why I do what I do.

The joy that I'm talking about here in this book is the joy I want you to find. This joy comes from living every second that we are gifted in being fully present in every moment.

There's a lesson I saw online a while back. It basically talked about how we are all allotted the same number of hours, minutes, and seconds every day. The problem is that a lot of us squander this most precious commodity - time. This problem is especially prevalent in our day and age, with the various technologies that we have at our disposal, technologies that give us instant gratification and distract us from focusing on a purpose. We are more prone to waste our days away on social media platforms, games, or even just regularly sleeping until noon. We waste time at work shopping or surfing the internet instead of doing work because these things are so captivating. They have influence and a strong pull. We end up not fully using the time we are given, instead it is squandered. It is empirical that we fully grasp the importance of living life and not just going through the motions.

Consider the fact that all of us have the same number of seconds in a day, but not all of us are promised tomorrow. For me, when I go to bed, I thank God for the day that I've had, rough or smooth, and I thank God in advance for the next day. I ask God for the grace to do what I'm supposed to do on this Earth and, for me, that is living life with a purpose and changing the lives of others.

My desire for you is that you find your joy beyond your cell phone and computer screens; go beyond your normal days, make one day not be a clone of the last. Find your joy - that hobby that makes you happy or something that you would pay to do simply for the joy it brings. Find that something that fills you with the sensation of completeness, so much so that you get lost in it and forget your troubles. It could be fishing or photography. It could be music. It could be a dream of yours that you believe in, something that you would love to spend your life doing. It could even be something as simple as a day at the beach, the sunset, or beautiful pictures of nature. Whatever it is that brings you joy.

Your time on this Earth is limited but purposeful. It is short but holds immense potential. We mustn't get too caught up in the troubles that life brings.

Understandably, a lot of people let certain experiences affect their general outlook on life.

Life comes with good things as well as bad and some of us let the hardship of life drive us to extreme coping mechanisms. Some people turn to drugs, alcohol, food, and other temporary solutions to escape from the world. The keyword in all this though is "temporary." None of those things offer lasting happiness or bliss. A more efficient way of coping with challenging times, as well as savoring the good times, is finding your joy.

You can even find joy in the littlest of things. If you have ever been in love with someone, you have probably noticed that you found almost everything about that person delightful, right down to the way they bite their nails or the way their eyebrows are a bit arched. That is the outlook on life you should aspire to have, to be in love with every single step of your day from the moment you wake up, to even brushing your teeth with enthusiasm.

The truth of the matter is that we must choose to create our own joy. If you decide that there is nothing in life that is enjoyable, I doubt there are many people or circumstances that can change your mind. True joy comes from within.

Once you find your joy, one of the most important things to do is to learn contentment. Think about everything you have ever wanted, whether big or small. Think of all the outlandish things that your wildest dreams can muster. Do you realize that you will never be genuinely happy with any of those things if you lack contentment? You could gain the entire world and then some, but if you are not content, you will never find peace of mind, happiness, or fulfillment.

What I want for you is to find happiness, and not just joy, but lasting joy. What I want you to do is think about the things that bring you joy. Find your joy and, whatever it is, write it down and paste it somewhere you know you will always see it. This way you can be constantly reminded to keep the joy in your heart.

Activity #4: What Brings Me JOY?

What would bring me lasting joy?

❖

❖

❖

❖

After you write down what would bring you lasting joy, number them in order of importance.

What is stopping you from having lasting joy?

❖

❖

❖

❖

After you write what is stopping you from having lasting joy, number them in order of importance.

CHAPTER EIGHT

Find Your Legacy

"Legacy" means different things to different people. Webster's Dictionary defines legacy as something transmitted by or received from an ancestor or predecessor or from the past. A legacy is also what you leave behind, what you built during your time, whether it be good or bad. For me, I see legacy as what I am leaving for the people that I serve and connect with in my life and the people that I love. Creating a strong legacy while I'm alive so that I can leave it when I am no longer on this Earth is important to me.

Here's the thing – throughout our lives our legacy can change quite a lot. It is okay that it changes. I recall a saying about legacies that goes, "It is all about the dash on the tombstone." The tombstone will have your birth date, a dash, and then your date of death (for example: June 1, 1935 – December 10, 2015). Usually written above and below this is something that speaks to the type of person someone was or the legacy they left; this is called the epitaph. The epitaph is the stuff that the dash stands for. Some people have "Beloved Father and Son" as their epitaph while others have beautiful words that describe virtues and life achievements, their legacies. The question is: What do you want to have written on your tombstone?

When I was a little girl, I wanted to be a nurse. I wanted, so badly, to help lots of people, and I thought being a nurse was the perfect way for me to do that. My grandmother worked at the hospital at the time. I saw her help a lot of people and I thought that was cool. I aspired to be like my grandmother. But, I had so many traumatizing experiences, experiences involving a lot of blood, lots of my blood. I came to realize that I am not incredibly good with blood. So, I decided that I no longer wanted to be a nurse. Sorry, Grandma. Even to this day, I don't like the sight of blood. It's just one of those things I cannot stand being around unless it's safely contained inside of me of course.

Now, what was I going to do? I mean, my nursing dream was dead and buried, but I still wanted to help people. That desire hadn't changed. So, I looked at other people in my life that were around me. I'm an only child and both of my parents are artists, so I tried to look for my creative bone. I struggled to discover my gift in art, and trust me, I tried many types, everything from drawing to sewing. I also tried everything I could think of that my parents did and were good at because that is what I had to emulate. I struggled and struggled to find what I was good at, despite all my efforts. I felt like a failure at everything.

It was challenging for me because, being a kid uncertain of the future and myself, I wasn't sure if I was ever going to find my way in life or figure out what I was supposed to do. This, for a lot of people, is what a legacy is. They find something inspiring that they can emulate, people that they respect and look up to. But the truth is that all those things don't really matter. Only you can determine your legacy.

Not too long ago I was speaking to my mom. We were talking about the importance of equality, among other things. She said to me that she's really blown away by all the things I have done because, when she was growing up, women typically went to college to get an "MRS degree," that is, to be get married and be a Mrs. When women went to college, education was a side note, because they really went to find their spouse. I could not relate to this because I found my spouse a bit late in life; I was thirty-six. I honestly thought I was going to be the single, old lady with cats and that was that. After going through some horrible stuff in life, I did not want to put myself out there. Happily, I did find a man that loves me and is good to me, so I consider myself to be very blessed for that.

So, for me, my legacy has evolved. I even found an art that I love to do, and am excellent at, making jewelry. Maybe you figured that out since my love for diamonds shines through. I also found a career in which I love what I do, being a financial advisor, a field few women are in. To illustrate an evolving legacy, let's use Nordstrom as a case study.

Nordstrom is a huge company that started in Seattle in 1901. It started by selling shoes, and that is what it was known for. Nordstrom was the largest independent shoe chain in the country. Eventually, the shoe store became much more. Nordstrom's customer service has become its hallmark. There is a story about people buying tires and returning them to a Nordstrom store in Alaska, and Nordstrom took them back. Were the tires bought at Nordstrom? No, Nordstrom has never sold tires! However, in every effort to deliver excellent customer service, they honored the return of the tires. Though it seems odd, it was a very strategic move to show their service model, a model that is still outstanding to this day.

Nordstrom bought Best's Apparel stores in Seattle and Portland and changed the name to Nordstrom Best, Inc. "Many people thought we were making a big mistake," said Elmer Nordstrom. Even the newspapers wrote us off. No one really believed that shoe store owners could be successful with apparel. No one---except us" (taken from Nordstrom 1991 Annual Report).

I tell this story because, in the city that I live in, the very first mall in the US was built, the Northgate Mall. The Nordstrom store that was there was called the legacy store.

Recently, I went to Nordstrom after it announced its closure because they were having a sale on all its furnishings and other goods. It was the store where I got my very first pair of heels; it was also the store where I got my first lipstick. It was also the store that hauled me in for shoplifting. I was shopping with a friend and had no idea that she had taken something. We were both taken in, and it scared the crap out of me. Thankfully, they soon realized I had nothing to do with it and didn't know anything, so they let me go. My friend was not so lucky.

Nordstrom has always been a part of my life, so, I wanted to get something meaningful at the sale. I tried to find one of those shoe size measurers called a Brannock Device. I clearly remember getting my first pair of shoes and the experience of having my feet sized. An associate put my foot down on the device and measured it to figure out exactly what size it was. Then, they went to the back room and returned with magical boxes of shoes. They put them on my feet so I could try them on. Over time, this experience has changed, yet to this day, Nordstrom still has fantastic customer service.

My Brannock Device (bought for $25) hangs on my office wall as a symbol of the excellent service I received. A client recently asked me if Nordstrom knew I had it? It's a great talking point. We had a good laugh and told stories about Nordstrom at the Northgate Mall.

As of now, the Nordstrom store is being torn down and the mall is being rebuilt into a new NHL practice arena. Even though the legacy store is being torn down, Nordstrom's legacy forever lives in my memories as well as the memories of many other customers. If you think about when the Nordstrom family built their store in the Northgate Mall so many years ago, I doubt they knew the impact their store would have. I doubt they knew what the legacy would be or how it would change and evolve. They have expanded to other regions. They have a brand new store in the heart of New York City. They have stores in Toronto, Canada where my stepsons live. They're everywhere now, even online.

So, when you think about yourself, about the things that you have accomplished, and maybe even failed at along the way, I want you to realize that your legacy can and will change over time. Just as your diamond is evolving into the shape, so will your legacy. As you connect with people, you are building your legacy. Just like my memories of Nordstrom, when you become part of people's lives and create a lasting impact, you leave a legacy behind that stays in their hearts. Make sure you are kind to other people and yourself as well.

Again, remember the dash on the tombstone. Even if your impact is not as apparent as your position as a beloved father, son, mother, etc. that, by no means, dictates the quality of your impact. It can be just as strong as a diamond. Diamonds are very hard to break. I want you to start thinking about your legacy every day because we are not promised tomorrow. What is the dash going to say about you?

If you died right now, what would be written on your tombstone? What would your epitaph say? How do you want to be remembered? Whether you are satisfied with your current legacy or not, your legacy priorities, know that you have the power to define it. At the end of the day, whatever is written on your tombstone is entirely up to you.

Activity #5: Tombstone Activity

If I were to die today, what would my dash say?

Am I happy with what it says?

What changes do I need to make?

For Your Notes:

CHAPTER NINE

Find Your Purpose

A lot of people act as if they were born with a little list that says, "Tiffany's life purpose is blah, blah, blah." They think that their destiny in life has been predetermined. I have a different opinion on the matter. I believe we find our purpose in life through unique experiences that help guide us in seeing what other people can't. Creative people are good at finding their purpose and, in turn, helping other people find their purpose.

Your purpose should not be limited to going to your 9 to 5 job that you hate. You might know the one? The one where you have to drag yourself out of bed and force yourself to go to a job you don't enjoy, doing the same thing, over and over again, every day. That's not your purpose, that's earning a paycheck! It doesn't always happen that our normal jobs exemplify our life purpose. For you, your life purpose could be a side hustle that you're involved in, something you love. It doesn't pay the bills right now but maybe it can one day. What if your purpose and earning a paycheck could be integrated?

I want you to think about your job. A lot of people don't pursue what their heart desires because they have a list of reasons not to. They think, "Oh, I'm too old," "I can't change anything about the trajectory of my life," "I can't go back to school," "I need the job I have right now," "I don't wanna do this," and "I don't wanna do that." Some of these excuses are understandable, but in the long run, none of them are valid reasons to not seek fulfillment in your job or personal life. I must tell you, all these excuses are only a result of your own mindset. Perception is key. The truth about life is that we all can do anything we put our minds to. Like it or not, what we brew in our minds, whether good or bad, manifests in our lives.

The world is filled with reasons for us not to be fulfilled or happy with our lives. Everywhere in society, including on social media, there are false perceptions of what happiness and fulfillment really look like. Every day we are fed ideas of a perfect body and a perfect spouse, a perfect job, a perfect bank account, and a perfect lifestyle and we soak it in without even realizing it. I'm not here to say these things are bad or unattainable. I'm just saying that they are superficial and don't give true happiness and fulfillment.

The sad truth is that a lot of us believe that these things will give us happiness. Because of this, we set these things as our goals instead of finding out what we actually want, what we actually love. This mindset is vicious because not only are these painted pictures of the perfect life false, they are unrealistic. It also doesn't stop there. The real damage occurs when we are unable to meet worldly goals. We end up hating ourselves and thinking the reason for failure is because we are incompetent or not as good as those picture-perfect people on the screens. We end up doubting ourselves and our worth. Even if we somehow get the things that they advertise to us as being parts of "the good life," we still don't find true fulfillment. It's no wonder why multimillionaires and famous people take their own lives. If money was the answer this wouldn't be the reality, but it is.

Instead of putting all your energy into superficial things, into telling yourself that you can't do this and can't do that, why don't you put your energy into things that YOU enjoy? Remember that our perception and our mindset create our reality. Just think about what you really want, regardless of how crazy you think it is. Put it out there to God or the Universe. Keep the thought or image in your mind; keep thinking about whatever that purpose is. Tell yourself the truth, tell yourself that you CAN have what your heart truly wants. You can study that course. You can get that job. You can get that promotion. You can get your dream job. You can start that business. All it takes is believing and the discipline to do what is needed.

Once upon a time, I told myself, "I can be a top wealth manager, helping as many people as I can, purposely changing one life at a time," and that's what I've worked toward. I've worked on this dream for years. I've been recognized by Seattle Magazine as a five-star wealth manager several times. I've also been recognized by my firm several times. These achievements didn't come easily. I had to choose to pursue them. I've been in the financial industry for a long time. It took immense courage to decide to go out on my own and do my own thing. It took tons of challenging work to bring it to reality. I didn't think I could do it, just like many of us who doubt ourselves and let fear stand between us and our dreams. I trusted God. I put it out into the Universe. I chased after it daily, and, thankfully, it came about. Was it easy? No. In fact, these types of things never are. Our dreams, desires, and purposes never come with ease but the Universe will rise to meet you. Just ask anyone who has ever done amazing things. They will tell you that they have had serious struggles along the way. The thing about those struggles is that your brilliance will shine through them.

I want you to figure out what your purpose is. Remember that only you can decide to do what you are meant to do. It lives within you and if it is not given life it dies with you. Achieving your purpose might take longer than you expect, but remember, all good things take time. Take time out of your day, every day, to think about your goals and aspirations and write them down. I use a journal to write them down. Some days I write a lot and other days not so much. If you do this, over time you will see common threads. The journaling is for you and you can write whatever you want. Think about the things that you love. At your job, the highlight of your day might be doing spreadsheets, and you really enjoy it, but maybe you don't like talking to people. Maybe it's the reverse. Maybe you really love talking to people and getting to know them, love helping people, but you also have to do spreadsheets, which you don't enjoy. Either scenario would suggest that you're not working in your sweet spot; you are not fulfilling your purpose. The Harvard Business Review defines the sweet spot of a company as: "...where it meets customer's needs in a way that rivals can't, given the context in which it competes" (June 10, 2008). You are your own brand with your very own purpose. Much like a business, build a brand and company around your brand.

Your purpose is something sensationally delicious and fabulous, like a nice piece of chocolate. It is so delightful and enjoyable, and at the same time, solves many problems in your life, including financial ones. If you can find the one productive thing that makes you feel that way, that is your purpose. Your purpose makes you feel like that piece of chocolate that you savor, or whatever it is that you have a taste for. This is what I want for you, this is what I want you to want for yourself. I want you to wake up with joy, anticipation, and excitement for the day ahead of you because you know that you have found your purpose.

CHAPTER TEN

Find Your Gratitude

Gratitude and thankfulness are immensely powerful concepts. Yes, they are feelings, but they are also much more than that. Did you know that one of the things that make us most happy as humans is showing gratitude to the people we are grateful for? The act of letting someone know that we appreciate them and the things they've done for us is a powerful instrument for finding happiness. But, since this is true, why stop there?

If you're reading this, I assume that you have some ability to read and understand words. Isn't that something to be grateful for? They say, "We don't know what we have until it's gone," but knowing this, what's to say that we have to lose what we have before we can appreciate it. Often in our lives, we feel like things couldn't be worse. The truth is things can always get worse. Instead of dwelling on the things that we lack, instead of homing in on the things going wrong in our lives, why don't we look around and be grateful for the privileges we have. We live in the most comfortable era in human history. If you are reading this in America or any of the Western or first world countries, chances are you're living in the best conditions that the world has to offer. So, look around you and see the things that you should be grateful for.

You have technology that makes virtually everything easier. Early humans used to spend most of their day roaming and hunting for food. Today we can order food on an app and have it delivered in minutes! We live in an age where boredom is a bigger reality to most of us than hardship. If born in the right body, at the right time, you could've been a slave, a trafficked and prostituted child, or so many other things. Yet here we are, binging on the latest Netflix show and ordering pizzas from the comfort of our couches. Then again, it doesn't really matter where you are or what situation you're in so long as there is air in your lungs and blood flowing through your veins. These are things to be grateful for. I want you to think about the things that you are thankful for and write them in the space provided below on page 99. It could be simple things like being grateful for water to drink, clean clothes to wear, or a roof over your head. The truth is that a lot of the people we share this Earth with don't have the simple things that we take for granted.

Millions of people live with an inadequate amount of food and shelter, sometimes none. Many people are completely helpless and must beg to get their next meal. Look around you. I guarantee that you will have something to be grateful for! The clothes on your back, the warm bed you get to retire to when the day is done. Be thankful for the food you eat; pour yourself a glass of water and drink it with gratitude in your heart because you are lucky to have that privilege. Be grateful for the money that you have, however little, however abundant. Realize that money is a tool, not a god, and be grateful that you have it.

Activity #6: Thankful/Grateful List

What am I thankful or grateful for?

❖

❖

❖

❖

I write this as my 50th birthday approaches and I'm grateful for all the years that I've been alive. All 50 years that led up to this moment, all 365 days a year, all 24 hours of every day I've been alive. I am grateful for each moment. Money can't buy time, nothing can, but I have been abundantly blessed with it, and I am thankful. Have there been terrible and challenging times along the way? Oh yes! Will there be more things along the way for me to combat? I'm sure there will be. But if I live beyond this moment, long enough to see those troubles, I will choose to be grateful for my life.

And you, the one reading this right now, you are still alive. I know life can be exhausting, and I know that you might be struggling with something right now. I have had my fair share of grief and, as every other person has, I struggled. For some, journaling helps, for others, speaking to God, for some meditation. When you're extremely low, remember that you woke up. That means you have more to accomplish. You still being alive is not a mistake; it's not just about the longevity of your brain and heart function or the fact that you can even breathe in and breathe out. God and the Universe are not done with you. Knowing this, you have more to be grateful for.

I must tell you a secret: it's not for us to decide when our time is up. We don't know when our last day on Earth is. I used to think it would be cool to know when I was going to die, and I imagine many other people have had this thought as well. I thought that knowing this would give me some sort of power, power over my life, the power to brace myself, and even the confidence of knowing with certainty when my life would NOT end. But now I realize that knowing this would be extremely ominous, I realize that it would be too much information to handle. I don't think anybody would want to know if they understood what knowing entailed. Imagine if you had a terrible fate. You would spend every moment before the actual event in agonizing fear, torture worse than fate itself.

The beauty of life is that it ends; that's what makes it so precious. We must live life knowing this and appreciating every moment that we have. We need to be thankful for the most precious gift we have, life. Be grateful for this day; be grateful for this moment.

The truth is that we won't have the people that we love forever; you never know when it will be their last day either. This is especially important because a lot of us seem to forget that tomorrow isn't guaranteed for any of us. We hold grudges with the idea that they will sort themselves out eventually. We let petty things like pride prevent us from fully appreciating the people around us. We're exceptionally good at doing this with the people that we love the most. Perhaps this is because they can hurt us the most, perhaps it's because we are desensitized to their presence and forget how much we need them.

The bottom line is, we tend to not appreciate the people in our lives. I want you to take the time to tell those you love that you love them. Tell them how much you're grateful for them because you never know when it's your last chance to do so. You never know when the last time you're ever going to see someone is because life doesn't wait for us to get our affairs in order. You don't want to lose them never having said, "I'm sorry," or "Thank you."

So, first I want you to learn to love and appreciate yourself. Be kind to yourself and celebrate your gifts. Even beautiful people feel insecure about their bodies. In contrast, there are traditionally unattractive people who couldn't be happier. I want you to be grateful for who you are. Be thankful for every flaw, every curve, and every line. If other people appreciate you, that's great, but if you don't appreciate yourself, all the love and adoration in the world is pointless.

This is where you start, by loving and valuing yourself. I want you to wake up excited and grateful that you woke up when many didn't. I want you to see your potential, even when others don't. I want you to see every day you get to experience as a gift, to see the present for what it is, the present.

For Your Notes:

CHAPTER ELEVEN

Scars: From Flaw to Beauty

Scars are proof that you are stronger than what tried to hurt or kill you. I used to be embarrassed by the physical scars that people could see. I have one right above my eye and multiple others on my body. I always tried to make sure that my bangs covered the one above my eye because I didn't want to talk about what caused it. Just like many other people, I felt embarrassed by it.

The thing that bothers me the most about my scars is not how I usually feel about them but rather what other people think about them and how they think it is okay to talk about them. The way they start a conversation about my scar is not always in the most flattering way. Over time, I've learned to be proud of my scars because they didn't kill me. I may have been hurt at the time of the injury, but not today. Today they are part of me.

The way people look at scars or visible disabilities is just their perception. It's their uncertainty, their fear, and their view; it's all about them. What they see has nothing to do with who you are. If we get lost in what other people see in us, we lose sight of the perception that matters, our own. Knowing who you are, your true worth, is more important than any opinion from onlookers. You should never forget that you are an original work of art. If they aren't insightful enough to appreciate it, it's their loss.

When people ask me about the scar above my eye, I have sometimes wanted to tell them fabulous stories about how I got it to make the story more interesting. I mean, the story is a bit embarrassing. I was racing for a swing with another girl, trying to get to it before her, and she tripped me and fell on top of me. Together, we slid into a two by four and it slammed against my face, from my chin up to my forehead! Thankfully, it missed my eye and went right into my forehead, all the way down to my skull. I bled and bled; my mom couldn't tell if the two by four had gotten my eye or not. Eventually, she found the wound, filled with the blood, of course.

So, see, it is kind of an embarrassing story; I got tripped by a girl fighting over a swing. I was in the lead, and she didn't want me to win. She came out without a scratch on her and neither of us got to swing on the swing we both so desperately wanted!

Most of my other scars are hidden by my hair. You do remember the story about the sledding accident, don't you? Those scars are immensely powerful; one is a huge, deep scar. I have dear friends that have other types of scars. Skin cancer scars, breast cancer scars. I have a friend who has scars from when she slit her wrists; she tried to bleed herself to death because she thought she wasn't good enough. Knowing people feel this way about themselves breaks my heart; that is why I think this chapter is crucial. Your scars are so much more than what meets the eye. Her scars symbolize a second chance at life because, if she had succeeded, her life would have been over. A scar can either shame you or remind you that you are blessed to be here, to have survived.

When you look at your scars, find the beauty in them. Think about what it took for your body to heal them, just the physical part alone. The process of your body having to mend layers of damaged tissue, the incredible feat that your body went through to heal you. Our bodies are masterpieces. Regardless of what you might think of your own body, none of it is a mistake.

There's an emotional side to scars that doesn't always heal as fast or as easily as the physical. Remember when we talked about diamonds? Your scars are also a part of your faceting and flaws, both parts of the beautiful diamond. Your faceting and flaws are there for a reason. There is a lesson in them. The lesson might not be just for you, but also for the people who can benefit from your experiences. You need to see the lessons and the beauty of your scars; appreciate the healing and recovery process they went through. While you might not entirely agree with this, you need to be grateful for your scars and to forgive; especially if they were inflicted by someone who abused you. So many people harbor anger against people that abused or hurt them whether it was physically, mentally, or emotionally.

One of the essential lessons in life is the truth behind forgiveness. What you need to realize is that forgiveness is not about the person that hurt you, it is about yourself. The more you harbor hate in your heart, it doesn't hurt the people that hurt you; it only hurts you. I urge you to find a way to forgive, to let those chains of hate go and be thankful for the diamond facets that you acquired from those difficult times.

You might not know it right now, but there is a reason you went through those things, a reason you experienced such turmoil. In five, ten, or maybe even twenty years, you're going to be able to help someone because of what happened to you.

Be cautious when you ask people about the physical scars that you see. Right now, I'm okay talking about mine, but I wasn't always, and not everybody feels the same way I do. Remember that you may not see what someone has or is going through. We're all being faceted in life, coming into our shape. It's not easy, sometimes it's painful. Use your words cautiously, because, just like everyone else, we don't know until we know.

Your scars are just another facet in your diamond; the important part is that whatever caused them didn't kill you, you survived and overcame.

For Your Notes:

CHAPTER TWELVE

Childlessness: From Flaw to Blessing

When I was twenty-two years old, I was given some devastating news. I learned that I would not be able to carry a child to term and, if I did get pregnant, I would have to abort the child. Granted, at twenty-two, I had no prospects for a spouse. But, like most girls, I always wanted to be a mom. For years, I had wanted to be a mom, or at the very least, have the choice. This news left me in a terrible wave of depression. I guess I felt like less of a woman because I couldn't do the one thing a woman could do that a man couldn't, the one thing that women dream of doing, have a baby. This news made me feel deeply flawed in the most intimate of ways.

I struggled with my inability to have children for years, as you can imagine. I figured that no man would ever want to marry me because I couldn't have his baby; in truth, I felt much less valuable as a woman. I went through a rough patch of dating for a lot of years. You see, whenever I would get close to someone and things would start to get serious, I would always sabotage the relationship in some way, I would always make it fail. I wanted these relationships to work and yet I purposely made them fail. It's a weird flaw to have, isn't it? Somewhere deep down, I thought of myself as undeserving or unworthy. Deep down I told myself I was incomplete without this one pivotal ability a woman should naturally have. So, I would wreck any chance I had at a lasting relationship.

Another trial that stemmed from this flaw of mine is that other women couldn't understand the depth of personal anguish that was rooted in not being able to bear a child. The depth of my shame was invisible to them. Sometimes I felt like I had no companion in this struggle because all the women that would naturally understand my problems could not relate to me. Up until I met my husband, I always heard things like, "Well you can have a child on your own," "Why don't you do 'this'?" and "Why don't you do 'that'?" Everybody was so ready to give me options in the form of compensation. The truth is, I didn't want to get into the reasons why I couldn't have a child. I was convinced that I was a failure as a woman and as a potential partner, that my body had failed me, and I it.

It's sad that, we as women, tend not to support each other in our decisions, whatever they may be, regardless if we agree with them or not. When I don't want to tell people the reason why I don't have kids, I say "Well, it just wasn't right for me." I make it sound like it was entirely my choice.

You see, we need to understand that women who don't have children, who are childless either by choice or by uncontrollable circumstances, are not any less women. If you are in a comparable situation, I want you to know and understand this. Your ability to have a child does not define your womanhood.

You also are not any less of a woman if you choose not to bear children. I was caught up in this idea for so long. It led me to depression and self-sabotaged relationships. I wish I had understood this back then because I would've saved myself a lot of heartaches. Having gone through it myself, I want to help whoever needs to hear this; a baby does not define you as a woman.

God does not make mistakes. I want you to repeat and meditate on this because it is essential. Whether you were born with flaws that leave you unable to give birth, you were born with mental issues that leave you misunderstood and confused, or born with a disability, remember that God doesn't make mistakes. You were made perfectly, with flaws, on purpose. That means that whatever the issue is that you must live with, something you see as a burden, if not a curse, God has a purpose. God always has you in mind, so don't be wary. His grace transforms experiences for the betterment of us and the people around us, we must have faith and trust Him.

You see, the man of my dreams already had two boys of his own, so I became a stepmom, and that was a whole other challenge on its own. Years later, things are definitely better, but in the early stages, life wasn't so rosy. Mother's Day has always been hard for me. In the early stages of being a stepmom, I didn't get recognized by my husband or my stepsons, and it was difficult.

In my career, with the job that I do, I have a lot of clients, and it's adorable because a lot of them started calling me Mama Money. One of them, who was in her nineties, even said, "You know, you're like my mama. You always make sure I make the right decisions, and you take good care of me." So, after that, I embraced the "Mama Money" thing. Now, people call out "Mama Money!" and I smile and welcome it.

From this experience I learned that being childless could be a blessing, because a lot of my clients see me in a mothering light. I embrace that I am a mama. I'm not just a mama to my stepsons, I am also a mama to my clients. The fact that I didn't birth any babies doesn't make me any less of a mama. For the women out there who haven't had children due to personal choice or life being what it is, unfair, I'm sure you're a mama in some way. Please choose to see your childlessness as a blessing. We, women, are nurturers, so it's no wonder most of us feel like we need to birth or raise a child to feel complete. But the truth is, whether we give birth or not, we are still women and that is precious.

Even for men that haven't had the chance to have a child, or are unable to, I'm sure there are some feelings of loss. I imagine that the choice to procreate being taken away is hard on anyone. But remember that these are just flaws, they are part of what makes us who we are. The journey that we take in life is dependent on our outlook. There's a reason for everything, there's a message in every trial, there's a story unfolding in your life. I know it's hard to see the whole diamond when you are in the rough. That is why faith is crucial, especially in tough times.

For Your Notes:

CHAPTER THIRTEEN

Perfection? Not Even Close

The definition of perfection is the condition, state, or the quality of being free or as free as possible from all flaws and defects (www.lexico.com). So many people struggle with their self-worth. In fact, I don't think anybody is above this struggle. Maybe you don't strive for perfection, but you beat yourself up when you display flaws or make mistakes. But here's a little secret you already know: Nobody's perfect. We cannot be perfect; we simply are not meant to be.

What would you do if you knew you could not fail? Recently, I was at the Museum of Flight in Seattle, and I read that the Wright brothers created several different versions of gliders/airplanes before the final and best version took flight. Most people do not see the Wright brothers as failures today, but that is because they did not give up. If they had stopped halfway through their breakthrough, the odds are that none of us would know their story or their names today. But, unfortunately, oftentimes, we see ourselves as failures, even in small endeavors. We are afraid of the judgment of failure, especially since a lot of people out there are so ready to place judgment upon others and put people's dreams down. Spend some time on Facebook, and you will see what I mean.

At some point in our lives, someone will try to shut down our dreams, most likely because someone did that to them. It's not alright to do that, yet it happens repeatedly. You might even find that the effect is not as direct. As we get older, we tend to dream smaller, due to a variety of factors in play. Teachers tell us we're not good enough. We are silenced by incompetence constantly ringing in our ears, causing us to hide our creativity. We are discouraged from our big-eyed dreams because of the insecurities the adults around us have.

They call this "maturity" and "facing reality," but let's call it what it is shall we? The murdering of dreams. Some people are either lucky enough to have encouraging people around to support them or have the sheer will to refuse to give up their dreams; these are the people that find fulfillment and success in their respective endeavors. Regardless of whether you have pursued your endeavors or your dreams have been shut down, irrespective of your experience, let's break the cycle. Let the murdering of dreamers stop with us. When we see people express their ambitions and dreams, be the first to encourage them. Let them know that you can't wait to see them at the summit of their respective mountains, regardless of where you are on yours. Don't let your insecurities, if any, extinguish someone else's fire. If anything, let their light encourage you to dream as well. Be the change you want to see in the world.

People also have a habit of trying to perfect themselves. It's a common trend in our day and age, an age where we have the technology to fix most of the things, we don't like about ourselves. We can get a facelift to counter our aging skin, makeup to hide or correct our facial imperfections, you fill in the blank. Many people think that a million dollars in the bank will somehow make their lives perfect. But, doing what I do, I see a lot of people that have way more money in the bank than they know what to do with and they're still not happy. I've also seen people with only enough to get by and they're quite content.

Now, I'm not saying that makeup or plastic surgery are terrible things, they're just tools. While these tools can be useful, they can prevent us from maturing into a state of contentment and appreciation for ourselves. For example, if you wear makeup to cover your freckles, it can make you feel confident when it's on, but it doesn't take away your insecurities. Same with money. Sure, it can make you feel better for a while, but the feeling is just temporary. If you can conquer your insecurities and be confident about your body or be content regardless of the amount of money in the bank, then your happiness is assured. Believe me, if you can master this concept and make it a natural part of your world view, you are much better off than the multi-millionaires who think that all they need to be happy is a bottomless bank account. Your happiness will have more longevity than the person who paid for the perfect body. The truth is that the pleasures that come from those things don't last; the only sustainable and renewable source of happiness is contentment.

A lot of people even think that finding "success" or money will grant them acceptance from people. But, if someone can't love you regardless of the scars on your body, the freckles and wrinkles on your face, or the amount of money in your bank account, then they're not worth your time and energy. The key to happiness isn't the abundance or lack of money. Money isn't the root of all evil; the love of money is. Wearing makeup doesn't make you insecure but wearing it to hide something does. The key to happiness is contentment. Be grateful in every moment.

There's this misconception that when we get everything we want in life; we will finally be happy and content. This concept is the most deceptive, and maybe the most dangerous, illusion that we fall for. You see, wants are never depleted. Whenever we want something and get it, other desires arise. It is an inescapable law of human nature. The idea that "When we fulfill all our wants, we will be happy," is a fool's errand because it will leave you seeking perfection that doesn't exist until the day you die. The sooner you accept that this is a lie, the better.

There was a study in a LinkedIn article (Ignatova, 2019) that showed that most women do not apply for a job if they do not have all the qualifications required for the job, whereas men apply for a job even if they have only about 60% of the requirements. When did we tell women, "You can't do something until you're 100% there?" When did we, as women, start believing that? When did men realize they could go for it whether they had it all figured out or not?

I'm out in public interacting with a lot of people, networking. My job calls for it, and it's just what I do, I get to know people. For those of you who don't know me, I'm a plus-sized woman. That's who I am and I own it. One time, I had this incredibly attractive woman come up to me. Honestly, this woman could've been on television, she really was stunning. After hearing me talk at a business event, she came up to me and asked, "You are so comfortable in your skin. How do you do that?" I was a little taken aback, to be honest. In reply, I asked her, "How could you not be? You look like you have everything together. You should feel like you can conquer the world." I mean, seriously! This woman was absolutely stunning and it hurt my heart that she was not comfortable in her own skin. Where I couldn't see any flaws, she saw plenty. While her flaws weren't visual, she felt so challenged by them that they made her insecure. She wasn't comfortable in her own skin as beautiful as she was.

I implore you to think about this. Whatever your flaws may be, whether it be your weight, a lisp, whatever it is that people judge you on at first glance, remember how amazing and rare you are. You are perfect just as you are! It is human nature to judge people and make assumptions based on our first glance. Judgment is everywhere. It is something we cannot avoid, regardless of our appearance. But you must remember, people are making judgments based on first impressions. People have judged me a lot; assumptions have been made about me that were not flattering or true. But, once they got to know me, they looked past my weight; they looked past my scars and other appearance flaws. The people who judged became the very individuals who tell me that they miss me when they don't see me for a couple of weeks; they want to be in my presence, and that makes me feel amazing. I had someone tell me once that she missed me so much and that she loved every inch of me. This was a beautiful thing to hear. She wanted one of my hugs, she wanted to be around me and talk to me, she wanted to see my smiling face, and...she loved every inch of me.

Since we can't go around trying to prove to people what amazing people we are, people will judge us. Don't let their judgments convince you that that is all you are. The opinions that really matter come from the individuals that know and love us, but most important, are our opinions of ourselves, our words become us. We need to learn to see and appreciate who we are, regardless of the perception of others. Some of the most seemingly perfect people in the world are also some of the most unhappy. So many rich, famous, and influential people in the world take their own lives, leaving us wondering.

I know the sudden news of American Fashion Designer Kate Spade shocked me and broke my heart. She was amazing, yet she struggled so much that she took her own life. She was extraordinarily successful in her career, which left a lot of people, especially those in her line of work, questioning and reevaluating themselves. She had a jewelry line, the quality of which I found inspirational and awe-inspiring.

What this tells us is that perfection is not the source of happiness or even contentment. This also tells us that our perceptions of ourselves are the ones that matter the most. No matter the insults, if we take our own lives because of them, it wasn't the words that killed us, but the fact that we took them to heart and believed them. No matter how many compliments we receive, if we see ourselves as unworthy, that will become our reality. We shouldn't pursue the unachievable image of perfection blindly. What is perfect is the day and moment you realize that you are perfectly flawed.

CHAPTER FOURTEEN

Forgiving Your Flaws

This chapter is a tough one, but its importance outweighs its uneasiness. Do you know all the things that faceted your diamond, particularly the people that hurt you? A lot of us, myself included, have been mentally, physically, or sexually abused, controlled, and belittled by others. Well, now is the part where you address that pain. It is the time where you need to find forgiveness in regard to those situations.

Let me tell you a little story about forgiveness. I've always had an interest in rocks, just like I've always liked jewelry. When I was a little girl, I had this neighbor who had beautiful little rocks. I thought they were cool, all sorts of neat. There were different shapes and sizes, and I was in love with them. She lived just a couple houses down from us. One day I remember I was at her home just having an enjoyable time. I was looking at the rocks, fascinated by them as usual, and I stole some. I put them in my pocket, and I brought them home. As I was trying to look for a way to display the rocks, I told my mom they were a gift even though that wasn't true. Mind you, I was young at the time, probably six, maybe seven years old, but I was so excited about these pretty rocks because I loved them and wanted them.

The funny part is, if I had asked the woman, she probably would've given them to me, but I didn't. Of course, my mom knew she hadn't gifted me the rocks, so she made me go over to the neighbor's house with her to return them and to apologize. The woman said, "Oh no. It's ok. I really don't care. If she wants them, she can have them," but my mom said, "Nope, she can't have them." I was distraught, of course, but I apologized and asked her for her forgiveness because what I had done was wrong.

I knew what I did was wrong and that I had to apologize, not only to my neighbor but also to my parents, and I did. My parents forgave me, and the neighbor lady forgave me as well. Yet, I was still racked with guilt; I was frustrated and uneasy in my heart. My mom told me that I had apologized to both her and dad, and I had apologized to the woman I stole from, but maybe the person I hadn't apologized to and asked for forgiveness from was God. I looked at her with my big eyes full of tears, so distraught, so unhappy. I was a pretty joyful little girl so for me to be like that, you know how serious it was. I marched right into my room and did precisely that. I went and I talked to God. I apologized, and I asked for forgiveness, and I felt like a weight was lifted from me. It was as if the weight of the world was lifted off my shoulders; the guilt was gone.

I had completely forgotten about this story until I was talking to my mom and dad about authoring this book and they brought it up to me. That's the fantastic thing about forgiveness. I had forgotten about that story completely; I had forgotten about that whole situation. When my parents reminded me, it took a little bit of digging, but I did recall it. What I remember most was the sense of joy that I had when I came out of my room after talking to God. I was simply happy again. So, when you wrong somebody, no matter how hard it may be, apologize and ask for forgiveness, from them and God. You might not get the reception that you want, and you might not even be forgiven. But if you are genuinely sorry for what you did and you apologize, you have done what you can, the right thing.

Years ago, I sought out some counseling because I experienced something traumatic. I remember one of the things the counselor told me was to think about that memory as a movie film, like the reel-to-reel kind. The kind that if the film gets exposed to light or wet, it gets damaged or eaten away and you can't see what's on it anymore. The counselor made me think about what had happened. She made me visualize what had happened and then said, "Ok, so we're going to relive that again, but now there's been honey poured all over it. Can you still see it?" Of course, I could still see it, I mean it was just honey. But now, we were throwing dirt on the film. And next, oh, it accidentally caught fire and burned. The only things that were left were the film reels. The actual film was gone. There was just a pile of ash that I could just blow away, and it would be gone.

If you have things in your life that you can't seem to move past, write yourself a letter, or write the person who wronged you a letter. Stop and get several blank pages to write on, a pen or a pencil, and some tissues. Close your eyes, breathe deep, and repeat 5 times – "You can't hurt me anymore." Be prepared! Your eyes might leak; however, these are tears of strength and power. You are taking your power back! Open your eyes and write freely, without correcting the spelling or grammar...let it flow through you like water out of a faucet. Now that it is done

- burn baby burn - that letter. Make sure you burn it in your fireplace or somewhere safe. The last thing I want is for you to burn the house down. I prefer to burn letters like this so I can take the ashes to a large body of water and watch them float away!

Doing this activity is especially important if something was done to you that was not your will. The odds are that the people who hurt you aren't losing any sleep over it; they are living their lives carefree, while the only one hurting is you. So, you can dwell on an event that has already happened, hurting yourself over and over again through recollection and reliving all while the other person has completely forgotten about it, just as I did with the rocks I stole. The inability to let go of this event or memory will also most definitely have its effects on the people around you. If you dwell on these memories, they will affect the way you perceive the people around you and their actions and it will hurt your relationships the most. You will keep making the same mistakes, not trusting your loved ones because of the experiences you've had in the past. You might even find yourself unable to find someone trustworthy because past experiences are still damaging you, deep down you believe this life is what you deserve.

This is not what you deserve, getting so bogged down with negative thoughts of yourself, not truly seeing the beauty and the love that is there. Everything in life begins and ends in love. Be open to seeing it and changing your self-talk. You must recognize what you have been telling yourself. Use the activity below to help with this. If you need more space, grab your journal.

Activity #7: Your Negative Self-talk – Time to Let it Go!

What things do I need to stop thinking and saying about myself?

Where or whom did they come from?

What would it take to forgive?

You are not those horrible things and thoughts. It is time to change your thoughts and create an image of who you are really meant to be.

As I said before, your thoughts become your reality. But, you have the power to transform the outcome! For many years, I was told that I was stupid, lazy, fat, and unlovable, among other things. That film kept playing over and over in my head. Eventually, anyone who has been treated like that will start to believe it and think that of themselves. Whether they were ideas inflicted in your head by another person or your internal words beating yourself up, don't let those thoughts fill your mind. Thoughts are powerful, they can make or break you. Think about the things that you let exist in your head and decide if you want them there. You need to realize what they do to your confidence and how they affect your life.

Forgive the person who taught you those things about yourself, whether it was someone else or yourself. Let the weight be lifted off of you because it's not on anyone's shoulders but yours. Realize that the only thing tying you down to those memories and feelings is you. Remember that forgiveness isn't for the other person, but for you. Yes, you are the one that was wronged, but you are also the one that will carry the weight of the memory for the rest of your life unless you learn to drop the anger or sadness or resentment within you.

You are a fantastic person, and no event in your past should disrupt the shaping of your beautiful diamond or the relationships that are meaningful to you. Because you're the one doing the forgiving, the weight will be shed, and you'll come out a happy and light child.

For Your Notes:

CHAPTER FIFTEEN

You are Relentless

The Free Dictionary has a compelling definition of the word relentless. It means, "firmly, often unreasonably immovable in purpose or will or existing or occurring without interruption or end (www.freedictionary.com)." You are relentless. Almost everything in this book up until now has been centered on some of the challenges you may have gone through or may go through in the future and how to cope and live a happy life in spite of them. Now, to say that "you are relentless" means to keep moving forward with every bit of energy that you have.

A ninety-nine-year-old gal who I worked with once told me, "Tiffany, I'm tired, I'm ready to die." You probably think that given her age, it's not entirely unreasonable to feel that way, and it isn't. I said to her, "You know honey, I understand. However, at the same time, it's not your choice to decide whether it's time for you to die, it's God's choice. Since you are still here you have more work to do; you still have a purpose. You might not know what that purpose is right now; you might not know what it might mean for other people to still have you here on this Earth. There's more for you to do, and I want you to keep living every day that you can, and I want you to live life relentlessly." She recently passed away at a hundred and one; she was a lovely lady, and she stayed lovely until the day she died. She had two more years of life to live after we had that conversation. You must understand that when your life ends is about God's timing not about how you feel.

Just like somebody hurt you in the past, every action and inaction that we take has a ripple effect on the people around us; you need to think about the collateral damage. You may be tired of fighting; you may be tired of struggling through whatever battle you're in whether it be cancer or depression or insecurities. It could be the struggle of autism or dyslexia or bipolar disorder, or just being misunderstood by the people around you and the stigma that labels bring. But during all this, you must remember God doesn't make mistakes. There are people around you that still need you to continue your fight. You might not have even met these people yet but the fact is that God doesn't make any mistakes. God didn't put you on this Earth to suffer and doesn't allow you to go through hardships that you can't handle or bear. You are stronger than you think, so for the sake of the people that need you and the people in the future that will need you, you have to fight relentlessly, no matter what!

However, if you feel lost and need help there are people around you who can help you with what you're going through. It may not be the people that are immediately around you, because the people you are surrounded by could very well be the problem, but people who can help you are out there.

I'll tell you about an experience I had when I was in high school. I've always been a plus-sized gal; I wasn't as plus-sized as I am now, but, back then, it wasn't as common to see people who are overweight as it is nowadays. Back in high school, I think I wore about a size fourteen, I was big. I was well under 200 pounds, but since I was just a little over five feet tall it was a lot of weight on my frame. I've always been told, "But you have such a pretty face," by my family and friends. Part of me knows they mean that to be a compliment, but for another part of me, it also implies other things.

So, in high school, when it came time for nominating the homecoming court, most of the school voted for me to be homecoming queen as a joke. I knew it was supposed to be ironic because they also nominated the boy in the school that everybody teased because he always had greasy hair and was a loner, as homecoming king. As you might be able to imagine, it was hurtful and humiliating. Thankfully, I had some friendly teachers in the school. They made sure that my nomination was removed and, naturally, a gorgeous girl in the class was voted for. Still, the situation ended up being quite the joke, I was quite the jest. I continued to have to spend my days with the people that did this to me, every day. Back then, bullying was commonly discussed like it is now, but was not appropriately handled. I even got bullied by quite a few teachers in high school. The words that they used against me were not great.

However, deep within me, I was relentless. I was immovable in my will, and in my purpose, I was firmly planted. Did being bullied make me sad? Of course. I was being bullied by people who were around me all the time, and that could very well be the case for you as well.

When you're in situations like that, you need to find the people that truly love you, care for you, and support you; it doesn't matter how many there are. The truth is that they're out there, though sometimes they're hard to find. Whether you are being bullied in person or being cyber-bullied, there is help. Maybe you're dealing with drugs or alcohol or some other affliction and you feel like you need help. There are support groups that can help. If you're severely depressed, please talk to somebody, ask for help.

When you're going through tough times, when you feel like it's just you, when you feel like you're alone, remember that you are not alone in this world. You are not alone unless you choose to be! The truth is, there are so many people whose lives we touch in ways we don't even know.

Find your support, find your tribe, and find your relentlessness. Relentlessness is the ability to keep fighting and keep improving our human condition no matter what life throws at us. I believe that every single person is capable of being relentless, including you. You just have to find it within yourself.

I love the word 'relentless.' A lot of people think its negative, but it's not. It is so powerful. Imagine yourself as a warrior; an unwavering being that cannot be swayed by hardship; a person that falls, but gets back up stronger and more confident; a person with an unmeasurable will to keep fighting their battles, coming out on the other side a stronger person. I believe that that person is within you; I believe that person is you.

Think about your diamond. When a diamond is faceted, the parts that are cut off become diamond dust, exceptionally fine dust that sparkles as the light hits it.

Those parts were cut off you and turned into dust for a reason. Go out and gaze at the night sky, at the beautiful stars up there. There are billions of stars out there. If you need to jump into your car and head out of the city limits to see them, do it! Stars are everywhere, scattered beautifully across the sky. Now, imagine your diamond dust having been carried by air into the sky to be those stars. See all the lights? The sky would not be complete without them, just as you would not be complete without them. You are perfectly flawed and rarer than any diamond!

CHAPTER SIXTEEN

I Am

During the process of authoring this book, all the words that people have used to define me, all my past experiences and hardships kept coming up. While the process can be painful at times, it is also full of healing. We live in a time where technology, such as social media and the internet, are prevalent. Technology can be a wonderful gift and tool and also a very dark place. I have a lot of people on my Facebook page, both people that know me well and for a long time and people that I haven't known long at all.

One day I posted on my Facebook page asking the people that know me to post three words that they thought defined me. This made me feel very vulnerable and I was concerned. It's strange that even to this day I was concerned that the words I was going to see were "loud," "fat," "lazy," "unlovable." It's just weird what a person's mind holds on to. But I put it out there anyway, and the words that came back were amazing. "Lovable," "kind," "brilliant," "caring," "relentless," "integrity," "joyful," "giver," "friend," and it goes on and on, lots of beautiful words. I have collected them on a page.

Let me tell you a secret. There are a ton of people that want to be in your life, they want to be your cheerleader, they want to be around you, and they want to feel your energy. I have people that I haven't seen for just a couple of weeks. They'll call me up and tell me they just miss being around me. It's a wonderful feeling. You are those things to other people. Depending on where you are in life you might not have met them yet, or maybe you just don't see them, but they're there.

Ask your friends and family, whether it be in person, through email, Facebook, or whatever other social networks you use, what three words they believe define you. Give them time and then compile the responses.

Some of them might be rude, depending on where you post and who sees it, because, as I said, the internet can be a dark place. Luckily, when this happened to me, the people that I got the harsh words from did not surprise me at all. The benefit of getting those types of responses is that I know the people that I should keep at arm's length. If there are people who are not good people, who are not supportive, who always bring you down and make you feel horrible after you talk to them, then those are people that you need to let go.

The people who love and care for you and truly know you will surprise you with all the wonderful ways that they describe you. I know in my case, some people thought three words weren't enough, that they needed more. You might be reading this thinking that this happened because I have people that have wonderful things to say about me and you feel like that might not be the case for you. For me, there was a time when all I heard were the harshest of words, some from people that I cared for and deeply loved. The words were so hurtful that, even at the time I made this post, I still felt insecure and unsure about the responses I would get. But I also know that I would never have gotten to where I am today if I didn't decide to be relentless and fight through the tough times.

There are always going to be tough times, which is why you need to do this. The people that love you and know you will tell you the beauty they see in you, the beauty that you might not see in yourself. When challenging times come, it's almost magical how easy it is to forget all the wonderful things about yourself. However, if you ask others to remind you of your gifts when those troubled times come, you can always go back to the reminders of what a wonderful person you are!

You will be reminded that there are people who love you and see your potential. During the tough times is when you need reminded the most. I can't tell you how cool it's been to see people, especially the people that I haven't even known that long, connecting with who I am. They see me clearly for who I am which tells me that I'm giving off the right vibe. My magnetism and purpose are coming through to the people whose lives I've touched. Hopefully, doing this activity can inspire you the way it inspired me.

You'll be amazed at how many times you see the same words repeatedly. Those beautiful words are your power words; those qualities are the core of who you are. I bet that if you think about it, the qualities are who you believe you are too. I'm excited for you to do this!

Activity #8: Three Words

Who do I know that I feel I could ask?

Should I post the question on social media?

What were the three words that people listed? List them all and see what words are repeated. This is the really fun part.

What are the top three words that were used to define you?

1.

2.

3.

Do you agree with them? Are there any surprises?

CHAPTER SEVENTEEN

Fine? Really?

All too often we ask, "How are you?" We usually do this in passing without realizing that we are asking a real question. Almost always, when the question is asked of us, we answer "Fine," when, in fact, we are not. Some of us are even going through ridiculously challenging times.

We often do this because we don't want to say, or don't know how to express, what we are going through. The reason for this is because describing what is not fine in one's life can make one very vulnerable. Choosing someone to be vulnerable with, and trusting that what we share with them will not be used against us, can be quite a challenge. We may also run into others that respond that they are fine, when in actuality they are not. Allow them the same grace that you wish to have.

Remember that the faceting process happens to every one of us. Diamonds can cut and facet other diamonds, so your words are important tools for both building and destroying. We must be cautious with our words because the last thing we want to do is cut somebody down when they're going through a challenging time. There is a good chance that we don't know what they are going through, and they don't know what we are going through either. So, I'd like to challenge you to change your approach. Rather than asking the question, "How are you?" a better approach would be to ask, "How's your world?" "How can I help you?" or "What can I do to make your day better?"

It does take willpower to do this, especially since we might end up sacrificing time and energy, but I will tell you, it takes the pressure off of a lot of people. Think about the last time you were going through a challenging time and someone asked you, "How are you?" Was "Fine" the answer? Were you really fine? I mean, fine is great for describing wine, or a texture, but as an answer to how you are doing or feeling? I don't think it is good enough. What if they had asked, "How can I help you?" You probably would have breathed a sigh of relief, thought about it, and then answered.

A lot of times, people only ask how you are doing because they have their own agenda. They might ask you how you're doing only to hear you ask it back and then lay their problems on you. Sometimes they ask not even caring about the response. This is what I have the biggest issue with, that the question has lost its meaning. Instead of truly wanting to know how someone is and if one can help in some way, it has become an "it's all about me" question. If someone trusts you enough to share what is going on or ask you for help, thus being vulnerable, help them in some way. Ask them what help they need or what they need from you. Honor their vulnerability with love and grace. One day, you may need help and choose to be vulnerable too.

The thing is, in this digital age, we are prone to sending a text or an email instead of calling someone or visiting them. Most all of us have cell phones that have free long distance included - please call and see what you can do to help or see if you can stop by and give them a hug. This little step can mean the world to that person at that moment. We are all on this Earth at the same time for a reason; you are not alone.

Think with love, act with love, choose to love. That person you meet might be dealing with a terminal illness, mental illness, loss of a loved one, or so many other things. Maybe all they need is a hug, a shoulder to cry on, or an ear to hear, someone to listen to them. If we all realize that we are all in this world together and that we're all each of us has, maybe we would change the way we treat each other.

So, the next time you ask someone how they're doing, think about what you're actually wanting to ask. "How's your world?" "How can I help you?" "What can I do to make your day better?" If we get everyone to do the same, the world would be a much better place for all of us.

CHAPTER EIGHTEEN

Love Like There is No Tomorrow

Here are thirty seconds of truth for you: You were born, and you will die someday. You have something within you that only you have, something only you were meant to do. If you don't do it, it dies with you. Do it, and do it relentlessly, as if your life depends on it, because in a way, it does.

You are loved. Even if no one else tells you again in your life, know that you are loved, flaws and all.

Remember when I said that we all have the same number of seconds every day? All too often, when people are diagnosed with an incurable disease or are dying, and a doctor tells them, "You only have x weeks or months left to live," it is as if a stopwatch starts. They start telling their loved ones how much they love them; they start making things right with the people they care about. They have little to no fear about the reception, only that the message is conveyed before they are gone.

The truth is, the stopwatch started when we were born. It has been ticking away every second of every day of our lives. We often take the things that we love and care about for granted. We procrastinate and not only put off paying attention to our loved ones but also pursuing our dreams and purposes, sometimes throughout our entire lives. The only thing that changes when we are faced with our mortality is perspective. We obtain a sudden realization of what matters, how precious time is, and how easy it is to do the things we ought to.

What if you could somehow hack into the wisdom and clarity that only the threat of impending death gives? What if you started living each day fully present? What if you lived in the moment, neither in the past nor the future? What if you could live a life of quality, not filling time with futile things and thoughts, but with meaning, purpose, and love? Love really is the answer to everything. I implore you to live as if your very existence depends on the quality of love that you radiate.

Now, I'm not going to challenge your beliefs, however, whatever beliefs you hold, you will never again be who you are right now, today, at this very moment. There is no do-over for you. There is only one glorious you. You have the power to affect and change people's lives and, most importantly, change yours at the same time.

Love like there is no tomorrow. It may be, that, for you, tomorrow does not exist. We live our whole lives and the next day never fails to come. This leads us to feel entitled. But the truth that only a person on their death bed can tell you, is that tomorrow is truly not guaranteed for any of us, young or old, evil or kind. We should not be so naïve as to forget this reality, and not so unwise as to negate the importance that death gives life itself.

Considering this, I implore you to live like there is no tomorrow. This is not a call to find the pleasures of life and bask in them, but a call to sort out your priorities daily. What matters to you? What makes you happy and whole?

Activity #9: Love, Live, Forgive - Like Your Life Depends on It

What really matters?

What makes you happy and whole?

When you are done writing these down I want you to turn to pages 19 and 20 to see if these are the same things or if they are new.

I'm not trying to make things gloomy and sad, but I want you to understand just how short life is, just how fast seconds go by.

We are ever-changing and ever-evolving. Whether that evolution is for better or worse is up to us. Remember all the faceting we go through to be the diamond we are meant to be? Each experience we have creates another facet in our diamond. Whenever all the faceting is complete, we don't know how or when this will be, I believe that is when God, or the Universe, take us home. Until that time comes, please use the tools in this book and the activities to guide and help you. Find your fight, find your joy, and find your purpose. Most of all, love like there is no tomorrow.

Another message I want to clearly convey is to always be the change you want to see in the world. I wish, for myself, to change people's lives for the better, one life at a time, with the time I have left. I hope that I have, in some way, no matter how small, changed your life. I hope that you will change others' lives as well.

Besides remembering to love, also remember that you are perfectly flawed. I want everybody who is reading this to know that you are all fabulous! You are all a work of art made by God Himself and, as I said before, God doesn't make mistakes. He's too busy creating beauty. That is what you are, that is what he sees in you, and that is what you should see in yourself. See yourself as the diamond that you are. I know I have said this repeatedly, but it is worth repeating. You are unique and beautiful because of your imperfections. The pain we feel in the trials we have is what makes us beautiful. We all have times when we're depressed. Even if we know how amazing we are and that what we are facing is just a cut in our diamond, life can still be tremendously hard, I know this. Certain things will try to break us. Some will come awfully close, but we can't let them. We can't give up the fight. We must move forward with love, faith, hope, and gratitude.

Love always,

Tiffany

P.S. If you enjoyed this book and you want more tools to help in this process, please be sure to head over to my website and sign up for messages of support and love. The website also has information on how to book me for speaking engagements. If you have loved this book, I've been told I'm even better in person! Thank you for spending this time with me.

My website:

www.youareperfectlyflawed.com

Made in the USA
Monee, IL
04 December 2020